Around the World
Sports

Margaret Hall

Heinemann
LIBRARY

www.heinemann.co.uk/library
Visit our website to find out more information about **Heinemann Library** books.

To order:

 Phone +44 (0)1865 888066

 Send a fax to +44 (0)1865 314091

 Visit the Heinemann Bookshop at www.heinemann.co.uk/library to browse our catalogue and order online.

First published in Great Britain by Heinemann Library, Halley Court, Jordan Hill, Oxford OX2 8EJ, a division of Reed Educational and Professional Publishing Ltd. Heinemann is a registered trademark of Reed Educational and Professional Publishing Ltd.

OXFORD MELBOURNE AUCKLAND JOHANNESBURG BLANTYRE
GABORONE IBADAN PORTSMOUTH NH (USA) CHICAGO

Designed by Lisa Buckley
Originated by Dot Gradations
Printed in Hong Kong/China

ISBN 0431 15133 4 (hardback)   ISBN 0431 15138 5 (paperback)
06 05 04 03 02   07 06 05 04 03 02
10 9 8 7 6 5 4 3 2 1   10 9 8 7 6 5 4 3 2 1

British Library Cataloguing in Publication Data

Hall, Margaret
   Sports. – (Around the world)
   1. Sports – Juvenile Literature
   I. Title
   394.2'6

Acknowledgements

The publishers would like to thank the following for permission to reproduce photographs: Title page, p.11 Timespace/The Viesti Collection; p.4 RaviShenkhar-Dinodia/The Image Works; p.5 Schiller/The Image Works; p.6 Bob Daemmrich/The Image Works; pp.7, 15 © Nik Wheeler; p.8 Craig Prentis/Allsport; pp.9, 29 Neil Tingle/Action Plus; p.10 © Cathy Melloan; p.12 Paul A. Souders/Corbis; p.13 Neil Rabinowitz/Corbis; p.14 Jon Burbank/The Image Works; p.16 John Wisden & Co. Ltd.; p.17 © Nancy Battaglia; p.18 Gunter Marx/Corbis; p.19 Mike King/Corbis; p.20 Stephanie Maze/Corbis; p.21 Le Segretain Pascal/Corbis Sygma; pp.22, 23 © Victor Englebert; p.24 © Richard T. Nowitz; p.25 Bas Czerwinski/AP Wide World; p.26 Sovfoto/Eastfoto; p.27 Caroline Penn/Panos Pictures; p.28 Sean Sprague/Panos Pictures.

Cover photograph reproduced with permission of Michael S. Yamashita/Corbis.

Every effort has been made to contact copyright holders of any material reproduced in this book. Any omissions will be rectified in subsequent printings if notice is given to the publishers.

Contents

Some words are shown in bold, **like this.** You can find out what they mean by looking in the glossary.

Sports around the world

All around the world, people enjoy sports.
The kind of sports people play often depends
on what the land and **weather** are like
where they live.

People used to run or ride animals just to travel quickly. They only caught fish to eat them. Now running, riding animals and fishing are sports in many parts of the world.

Outdoor sports

People play or do many different sports outside. The kind of sports they do depends on the **weather** where they live.

Some sports can only be done outside when there is snow or ice. Sports like skiing and ice-skating started in places where it gets very cold.

Indoor sports

Some sports are played inside special buildings. These buildings have lots of room for **athletes** to play. There is also room for people to watch them.

Inside a **sports arena**, the temperature can be kept at a comfortable level. The **weather** outside does not matter. That means people can do many sports all year long.

Sports on land

Many sports are played on land, others in water. Sports like baseball, football and soccer are played on fields. Sports like tennis and basketball are played on **courts**.

Some land sports are played at a fast pace. People race to see who is fastest. Other land sports are played slowly, like golf. Players need time to play carefully.

Water sports

Sports like swimming and surfing started a long time ago. People who lived near water learned to swim to stay safe in the water. They found that they could also move along on the water on surf boards.

Sailing and **motorboat** racing are also water sports. Another water sport is water-skiing. Fast boats pull skiers through the water behind them.

Learning a sport

People often start to learn a sport when they are young. They can also learn new sports even when they are grown up.

Everyone needs to **practise** to become good at a sport. The more someone plays a sport, the better he or she gets at it.

Rules

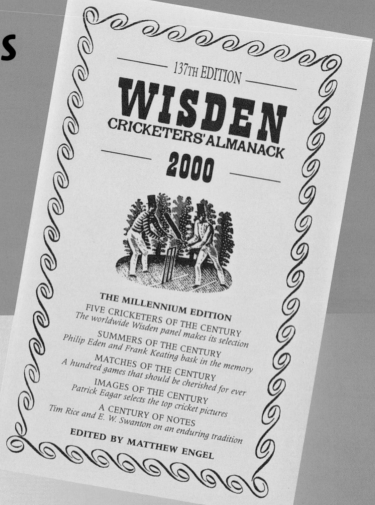

Every sport has a set of rules. Rules explain how players should act and what they should do. People who play sports have to obey these rules.

Some people have the job of making sure players always follow the rules. **Umpires**, **referees** and judges tell players if a rule has been broken.

Sports contests

People often play sports in **teams**. The teams have **contests**. Most of the time one team wins the game. Sometimes the contest ends in a **tie**.

Some **athletes compete** to see who is better at a sport. Some people playing a sport do not compete. They do it simply because they enjoy it.

Sports gear

Some sports **teams** have special clothing.
Players may wear **uniforms** to show that
they are on the team.

Some sports are played with **equipment** like balls, nets, rackets and even **sabers**. Players may wear masks and gloves to help keep them safe.

Ball sports

Many sports are played with balls. Some ball sports look the same but have more than one name. A game called soccer in some places is called football in others.

Ball sports can be played inside and outside. They are played on fields and on **courts**. They can be played by **teams**, in pairs, or by just one person.

Sports on wheels

Wheels are used for **transport** and for sports. People ride bicycles for **exercise** or to **compete** in races. They ride mountain bikes over rough ground.

For some sports, people race each other on motorcycles or in cars. These races may take place on roads or on **tracks**.

Body sports

For some sports, the body is the only **equipment** a player needs. People who do sports like gymnastics and wrestling learn many ways to move their bodies.

Martial arts include sports like judo and karate. They began thousands of years ago as ways of controlling the mind and the body. Today, they are popular sports.

Sports for all

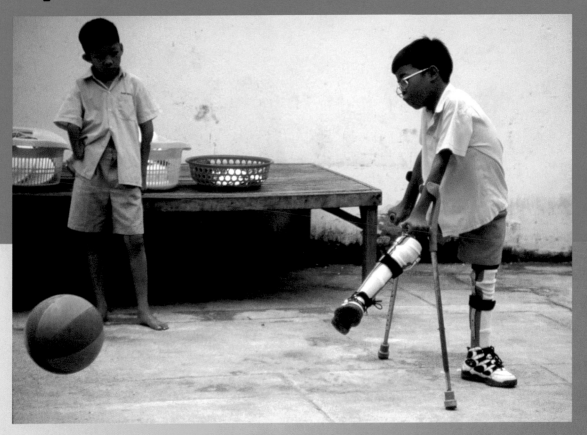

People with **disabilities** may use special **equipment**. They may play in wheelchairs. **Athletes** with disabilities often **compete** against each other.

Around the world, sports are alike in some ways and different in other ways. No matter where people live, many of them enjoy playing and watching sports.

Photo list

Glossary

athlete someone trained in a sport

compete to take part in a game against another person or team

contest game against another person or team

court hard playing surface

disability something that makes it difficult or impossible for a person to do an activity

equipment things needed to play a sport

exercise activities that keep a person's body in good shape

martial art art of self-control that is often done as a sport

motorboat boat that is powered by a motor

practise do something over and over to get better at it

referee someone who watches a game to make sure no one breaks the rules

saber sword used in the sport of fencing

sailing riding in boats that are powered by wind blowing against their sails

sports arena building in which sports events take place

team group of people playing together, usually against another team

tie score that is the same for two people or two teams

track round or oval surface for racing

transport ways people move from place to place

umpire someone who decides what to do during a game if players do not agree about something

uniform clothing that shows that a person belongs to a sports team

weather what it is like outside, including things like hot or cold air, rain or sun

31

More books to read

Going swimming by D. Church, Franklin Watts, 2000

Going to the match by Jonathan Shipton, FBA, 2000

Know the Game series, A & C Black, 2001

The football stadium by Carol Watson, Franklin Watts, 1997

Index